Faith, hope and love

Words of comfort in later years

To

....

From

....

Jarrold Publishing, Norwich

Breathtaking Highland beauty – Ben More, the highest mountain on Mull . . .

Acknowledgements

The scripture quotations are from the Revised Standard Version Bible, © 1946, 1952, 1971 by the Division of Christian Education of the National Council of the Churches of Christ in the USA, and are used by permission.

Faith

We talk of a 'faith that can move mountains'. There is a story that throws new light on that. A man was standing at the bottom of a great mountain. It would be good, he thought, to move that mountain into the sea. He picked up his shovel and began to dig. Two others came by and seeing the man at work offered to help. Soon others came, till a great army was digging away. At last the mountain was flattened – because one person had decided to make a start.

Jesus said 'Truly I say to you, if you have faith as a grain of mustard seed, you will say to this mountain, 'Move from here to there', and it will move; and nothing will be impossible to you.'

Matthew 17:20

. . . and Loch Cluranie, Highland

Small Things

Naaman was a great man. When he became ill he travelled to a far country in search of a cure. He was angry when he was told that all he had to do was dip himself in the muddy River Jordan. Then it was pointed out to him that he would have done some great and difficult thing willingly. Why not obey now, when all he had to do was wash and be healed?

Most of our lives, most of the time, are made up of ordinary, everyday events, the small things of life. We may yearn for big experiences or dramatic events to show our faithfulness. So often, what is asked of us is faithfulness in the everyday.

> *Well done, good and faithful servant; you have*
> *been faithful over a little, I will set you over*
> *much; enter into the joy of your master.*

Matthew 25:21

Durham Cathedral has stood on its rock above the city for nearly 900 years

Pretty Traitors Ford, deep in the heart of Oxfordshire

The River Nene flows smoothly past Fotheringhay, Northamptonshire

The Wondrous Cross

When I survey the wondrous cross,
on which the Prince of Glory died,
My richest gain I count but loss
and pour contempt on all my pride

Isaac Watts

It all began in a very simple way. Young Isaac had been complaining to his father about the poor quality of the hymns they had to sing.

'Then give us something better, young man.'

The challenge was taken up and that very day Isaac wrote the first of the hundreds of hymns composed before his death in 1748. Those of us who love singing hymns have Isaac Watts to thank, for he was the first to write them in any number. Of all his hymns, the finest is *When I survey the Wondrous Cross.* Indeed, many would rate it the best of all English hymns. And all because he accepted a challenge to do something rather than complain!

'I am With You'

The story is told of a young boy who belonged to a Red Indian tribe. He was very frightened because as part of his training for manhood he had to spend a night alone in the forest. He knew it would be very dangerous. Wild animals might spring on him without warning. Evil spirits would be prowling about in the darkness. There were traps he might fall into, dangerous swamps to suck him down. Fearful as he was, there was no way out of it. If he was to become a man in the tribe, he had to go through this test. With his heart in his mouth, he set out. All the long, dark night he walked the forest tracks. Every time a branch rustled in the wind or a twig fell from a tree he was terrified. But he plodded on and at last the dawn came. Suddenly he felt a strong hand on his shoulder.

'You did well, my son. Now you deserve to be called a man.'

It was the boy's father. The boy asked,

'How do you know I did well, father?'

'I was behind you, every step of the way.

Do you think I would let my beloved son walk through the dark forest alone?'

Jesus said, 'I am with you always'.

Matthew 28:20

A peaceful glade in Delamere Forest, Cheshire

Pulteney Bridge elegantly straddles the Avon at Bath

Steadfastness

Of all the qualities we may look for in a friend, surely steadfastness is one of the most important? That quality of loyalty which will stay by us through good times and bad. Others may be on our side when things are going well, but the steadfast one is there when we most need a friend – when we have made fools of ourselves, when our world is falling apart, when we feel the odds are against us.

If we have a steadfast friend, we know we are fortunate. If God is our steadfast friend, we are blessed indeed. And his friendship is ours for the asking.

> *I have trusted in thy steadfast love;*
> *my heart shall rejoice in thy salvation.*
>
> Psalm 13:5

Scott's Albert Memorial looks across Kensington Gardens, London

Windsor – the largest inhabited castle in the world

Only Praying

Cathie was feeling very burdened. Her family was going through sad times and she longed to support them. But she is old and not very strong and she felt she was more trouble than she was worth if she offered help.

'I am useless', she said to a friend, 'all I am doing is praying'. Her friend quickly responded.

'All you are doing! Why, you are doing one of the most important and positive things you could possibly do to help. Prayer changes things.'

> *Continue steadfastly in prayer, being watchful in it with thanksgiving.*

Colossians 4:2

Lochranza, Arran, is the setting for this tranquil scene

In Every Corner Sing

George Herbert could have been a rich and successful man. He was gifted and well connected and seemed set for a dazzling career in seventeenth century England. Indeed, his ambition was to be Secretary of State. But instead he became a country vicar and had to put up with hearing his friends telling him he was wasting his time and his abilities. The people of Bemerton may never have known about all that: what they did know was that their vicar was a good and holy man. When they heard the church bells ringing across the fields they called them the *Saints bells*. Living and working in his quiet parish he expressed his love of God in poetry. Some of the poems were later set to music and sung as hymns. It is as a poet and hymn writer that we honour George Herbert today.

> *Let all the world in every corner sing,*
> *My God and King!*
> *The heavens are not too high,*
> *His praise may thither fly:*
> *The earth is not too low,*
> *His praises there may grow.*
> *Let all the world in every corner sing,*
> *My God and King!*

Enjoying the beauty of Monsal Dale, Derbyshire

Cottages by the stream at Rockbourne, Hampshire

Trust

'If anything else goes wrong today I shall scream!' There are times when the whole world seems to be conspiring against you. Problems and frustrations mount up, disappointments meet you at every turn. Maybe you are attempting the impossible, or trying to do things you are just not made for, or is it that you are not feeling on top form and really need a rest? Letting off steam can help relieve the pressure – but do make sure no-one gets scalded in the process! Taking a cool look at where you are going may help. Just admitting that you are human and need a rest can sometimes be vital. Best of all, try trusting in the Lord.

Thou dost keep him in perfect peace, whose mind is stayed on thee, because he trusts in thee. Trust in the Lord for ever, for the Lord God is an everlasting Rock.

Isaiah 26:3-4

Boats at Bridgend, near Newton Ferrers in Devon

Faithfulness

How do you feel about your name? One of the advantages of an unusual name is that people remember it. Polycarp, for instance. You don't meet many called that, even though it is a saint's name! Polycarp was a Christian bishop in Asia Minor in the second century A.D. In his younger days he knew people who had spoken with Jesus. When he was very old a time of persecution came to the Church. Polycarp was persuaded to go into hiding but after he had had to change his hiding place twice, he refused to move again. So when armed police came searching for him he was not hard to find. He insisted on talking with his captors and feeding them and then asked to be allowed to pray.

After two hours, the police, now feeling very ashamed of what they were doing, took him back to the city seated on a donkey. He was manhandled into the stadium and the Roman pro-consul urged him to save his own life:

'Curse Jesus Christ and I will release you.' Polycarp gave his answer.

'I have served Jesus Christ for eighty-six years, and he has never harmed me. How can I blaspheme my King and my Saviour?' For that they burnt him to death.

Be faithful unto death and I will give you the crown of life.

Revelation 2:18

The Gothic splendour of Lincoln Cathedral

Wings As Eagles

'I haven't got the energy I once had.' It is tempting sometimes to envy the young as they gallop around. But even if our bodies are less active, our minds and imaginations can work as hard as they ever did. Some find themselves, for the first time in their lives, having the space to take stock and think through their beliefs. We shall not recover the physical energy of a youngster, but we are never too old to begin deepening our relationship with God.

> *He does not faint or grow weary, his*
> *understanding is unsearchable.*
> *He gives power to the faint,*
> *and to him who has no might he increases*
> *strength.*
> *Even youths shall faint and be weary,*
> *and young men shall fall exhausted;*
> *but they who wait for the Lord shall renew their*
> *strength,*
> *they shall mount up with wings as eagles,*
> *they shall run and not be weary,*
> *they shall walk and not faint.*

Isaiah 40:28-31

Orchard in full bloom near Sissinghurst in Kent

Hope

'There is still hope', we say, when the situation is bad. Then hope is like a little gleam of warming light. It saves us from despair. Hope means looking to the future. It means knowing that things can get better. It means trusting that they will. Hope is not always easy, which is why we should take opportunities to encourage each other in sad or difficult times. To help people to be hopeful is to be a witness to the love of God.

> *Blessed be the God and Father of our Lord Jesus Christ! By his great mercy we have been born anew to a living hope through the resurrection of Jesus Christ from the dead.*

1. Peter 1:3

Old-world charm at Chalfont St. Giles, Buckinghamshire

Heage Mill, Derbyshire

This unspoilt village street is in East Hendred, Oxfordshire

The Everlasting Arms

It was wartime, and a woman had to make a dangerous journey by sea. She was travelling alone with two very small children and was understandably fearful about how she could save them if the boat were attacked. Not long before she set out a letter came from her mother-in-law, who lived in the country she was to travel to but who could not have known about the proposed journey. One phrase in the letter helped the young woman find the courage she needed to face her ordeal. The message was 'Remember the Everlasting Arms'.

The eternal God is your dwelling place, and underneath are the everlasting arms.

Deuteronomy 33:27

A rainbow adds to the beauty at Craignure on the Island of Mull

Still Small Voice

Elijah was in despair. He had told people the truth about God's ways and they had rejected his teaching. Worse, they had turned against God and killed all the prophets except Elijah. He was in danger of his life and had hidden in a cave, thinking he might as well be dead. He needed, more than anything, a sign that God had not deserted him. There came a great, violent storm with a hurricane force wind, followed by an earthquake and then a fire. And then there was quiet, and in the quiet God spoke to Elijah in a still small voice the words of strength and encouragement he needed to hear.

For thus says the Lord God, the Holy One of Israel, 'In returning and rest you shall be saved; in quietness and in trust shall be your strength'.

Isaiah 30:15

The deep, sheltered harbour at Salcombe, Devon

Medieval St. Michael's Mount stands stark against the Cornish sky

The restored 12th century castle at Bamburgh, Northumberland

Too Busy

'I would like to do it, but I am too busy.' Business seems to be one of the besetting sins of our time. While a few find time hangs heavy, most of us rush from place to place in a mad way. In our hearts we know it is not good for us, yet it is hard to stop. And where in all the rush do we find God? If we dare to make time for God, choosing to set aside a few of our precious minutes for him, he will honour that trust. If the demands made on us are really so great that we cannot stop, he will understand that too, and meet us in the middle of the crisis.

It is the time to seek the Lord, that he may come
and rain salvation upon you.

Hosea 10:12

Baslow, Derbyshire

Loneliness

A shy little girl was finding her new class difficult. She did not seem to get on with the other children easily. They could not understand why she did not join in their games and chatter. While they were running around, having fun, she stood in a corner by herself, sucking her thumb. Seeing her loneliness, her teacher tried to find out what was wrong.

'I haven't got a friend' she said. The teacher took her hand.

'Oh yes you have. You've got me.' She began to play ball with the little girl. Gradually other children came and asked to play. There was soon a group around the child. She was relaxed enough to smile and begin to join in their shouting and laughter. Where once she had been on her own, now she was beginning to find friends.

Jesus said 'I have called you friends'.

John 15:15

Punting – the best way to see The Backs at Cambridge . . .

. . . and barging – on the Upper Peak Forest Canal

Enjoying the good life at Radway in Warwickshire

Blessings

'I like animals better than people.' That kind of remark seems deeply shocking to some folk. Maybe because it implies that the human race is hard to like. Or maybe because it suggests that the speaker has had bad experiences of fellow human beings. Either way it is sad to think of someone feeling so lonely. Caring for pet animals and enjoying their companionship should help make us more loving and sociable, not cut us off from our neighbours. Much better to give thanks for the love and loyalty and fun our pets give us – and then share some of that with other people.

Praise God from whom all blessings flow
Praise him all creatures here below
Praise him above you Heavenly Host
Praise Father, Son and Holy Ghost.

Bishop T Ken

The Blue Tit – a common and welcome visitor in many gardens

Amazing Grace

Amazing grace! How sweet the sound
That saved a wretch like me.
I once was lost, but now I'm found
Was blind, but now I see.

John Newton, born in 1725, described himself as 'once an infidel and libertine'. He went to sea at the age of 11 and drifted into a life of violence and wickedness. For some years he took part in the cruel trade in slaves. One day at sea his ship was caught in a violent storm and he thought he was going to drown. In panic he asked for God's help and believed his prayer was answered. He began a new life as a Christian and eventually, after many struggles and setbacks, became a clergyman. He wrote 'Amazing Grace' for his congregation at Olney. When he was over 80 he said, 'My memory is almost gone, but I still remember two things: that I am a great sinner and that Jesus is a great Saviour'.

Fishermen's boats at Cadgwith, Cornwall

Sunset over the ocean from the Island of Iona

Courage

Jane was born a spastic – her movements were jerky and her hands stuck out at funny angles. Her head seemed too heavy for her body. But she was not a sad person. The thing you noticed about her was her laughter. When she fell over – which was often – she treated it as a joke and expected you to laugh too. Her parents fought for her right to go to an ordinary school. With great determination, and armed with her hearing aid and typewriter, she kept up with the other children. Except for games. With the best will in the world she could not join in.

When the school Sports Day came round, Jane had to watch other children competing and collecting prizes. At last one silver cup was left. 'This is a new prize' said the headmaster. 'It is awarded to Jane, for great courage in the race of life.'

Let us run with perseverance the race that is set before us.

Hebrews 12:1

Spittal of Glenshee, Tayside

Bow Fell looms in the distance behind this Cumbrian farm

Buildings of the past: a splendid windmill at Burgh le Marsh, Lincolnshire . . .

Think about These

Sometimes the news seems filled with horror stories. Some days everyone we meet seems to have a depressing tale to tell. The good things we valued, the standards and qualities of life seem somehow spoiled. It is a good idea, when we feel surrounded by negative messages, to take positive action. We should look for beauty, or better still try to help create it. We should aim to be kind, faithful and courteous. We should encourage goodness in young and old and most of all in ourselves.

Whatever is true, whatever is honourable, whatever is just, whatever is pure, whatever is lovely, whatever is gracious, if there is any excellence, if there is anything worthy of praise, think about these things.

Philippians 4:8

. . . and the Oast House at Collier Street in Kent

Comfort

Martin Niemoller was a pastor in the German Church – and a fierce opponent of Hitler. His courage won the respect of many who hated what Hitler represented. By Hitler's special order he spent eight years in prison, four of them in solitary confinement. He was forbidden to speak to any of the other prisoners, but he discovered that if he put his stool on the table in his cell and stood on it he could just see the other prisoners exercising round and round the yard. He quietly read the Bible to them through his barred window. The word went round the prison that he was there. 'Martin Niemoller is here.' Even those who could not see or hear him were comforted. Just knowing that he was there with them brought comfort and strength.

Jesus said: 'I will not leave you desolate; I will come to you'.

John 14:18

Bustling shoppers at Cirencester, Gloucestershire

Enjoying the sunshine in the grounds of Winchester Cathedral

Cheerfulness

A bowl of flowering bulbs can brighten up a room wonderfully, particularly on a winter's day. The colour and scent counteract the greyness outside, and seem to bring a message of hope. No wonder the flowers are called 'Cheerfulness'!

A cheerful person can lift the spirits of a gloomy group. A mournful person has a depressing effect. We should ask for the gift of cheerfulness, because to be cheerful is to be hopeful, and hope is one of the great virtues.

> *A cheerful heart is a good medicine, but a*
> *downcast spirit dries up the bones!*
>
> Proverbs 17:22

Aconites and snowdrops bring cheer to the winter garden . . .

. . . and the crocus follows in early spring

Time stands still at Upper Slaughter in Gloucestershire

Love

Love is the highest gift of God; humble, gentle, patient love. All visions, revelations, manifest- ations whatever are little things compared to love.

John Wesley

John Wesley spent more than fifty years travelling throughout eighteenth century Britain, usually on horseback, to 'offer Christ'. His burning ambition was to help others to find the Christian faith, the royal way of love. He said that the world was his parish and that he came to bring 'plain truth for plain people'. He is honoured today as the founder of Methodism, for the power of his preaching, for his concern for the poor and for the hymns he and his brother Charles wrote.

The medieval arches of Stirling's Auld Brig, crossing the Forth since 1415

The Voice

Some sixty or more years ago a little girl was given the job of bringing a flock of sheep home. She had grown up on a farm and so was well used to the task and knew what was expected. As she came along a narrow lane on her way she met a boy bringing another small flock of sheep in the opposite direction. The sheep intermingled and the boy burst into tears. He could see no way of separating the two flocks and was horrified at the possible consequences. The girl said:

'Don't worry. I know what to do. Just watch.'

She walked through the two flocks of sheep, calling as she went,

'Come with me, my darlings'.

As she walked through the flock her own sheep followed her voice and so she was able to bring them safely home.

> *My sheep hear my voice, and I know them, and they follow me; and I give them eternal life, and they shall never perish, and no one shall snatch them out of my hand.*
>
> John 10:27-28

Summer grazing on Fontmell Down, Dorset

The Greatest of These

She had seemed such a quiet, gentle person all her life. Her name was never in the newspapers: her neighbours knew her, and the people she worked with, but outside her small community she was unknown. But those who did know her – her family, her friends, her colleagues, members of her church, neighbours, the newspaper boy, the people who served her in the shops, the young unmarried mother, the crusty old widower, the lonely little girl – they knew she was like gold. Not perfect, for only one of us was ever that, but kind and generous, thoughtful and sensitive and sometimes very funny. Above all, she had a way of making you feel better. Someone said of her, 'It was as if the sun came out, when she came into a room'.

When she died, the church was crowded for her funeral. Her family wondered why so many had come. The congregation recognised each other with surprise. Then they understood. They had all – young and old, family and stranger – been drawn within the circle of her love.

So faith, hope, love abide, these three; but the greatest of these is love.

1. Corinthians 13:13

Swimbridge Church, North Devon

The richly coloured, daisy-like blooms of cineraria

A Birthday

A birthday should be special, marked out for the individual in some way. Whether it is spent in the heart of a family, or quietly on your own, you should celebrate.

Celebrate the gift of life, because it *is* a gift.

Celebrate the knowledge that God knows you personally and you are uniquely precious to him.

Take stock, look back down the years you have come through and look ahead, though the future is always a mystery. Whatever lies before you, you need never travel alone. Jesus will be your constant, unseen companion every step of the way if you will ask him for his company.

Celebrate that!

I am like a green olive tree in the house of God.
I trust in the steadfast love of God for ever
and ever.

Psalm 52:8

Fulling Mill, Alresford, Hampshire

Grey Days

We all go through times of trouble and anxiety when we don't know which way to turn for help. The days can seem grey and hopeless and at night we toss and turn and long for sleep to come. It can be doubly hard if we feel we are facing problems alone. How comforting then to remember that God knows all about us, and cares about our troubles.

If I take the wings of the morning
and dwell in the uttermost parts of the sea,
even there thy hand shall lead me,
and thy right hand shall hold me.
If I say, 'Let only darkness cover me,
and the light about me be night,'
even the darkness is not darkness to thee.
for the night is as bright as the day;
for darkness is as light with thee.

Psalm 139:9-12

Lewis Castle, Stornoway, Lewis

Quinag from Unapool, Highland

This corgi looks hopeful – perhaps we're going for a walk? . . .

Companions

I met them out walking, the woman and her dog. She led a lonely life in some ways but her little dog was her constant companion. She told me what the dog meant to her. How he got her out of the house and taking exercise, even on days when she was tempted to shut herself away. How he was someone to talk to and fuss over in her otherwise empty house. How, when she was going up to bed, his bright, friendly face encouraged her up the stairs. And then it was a comfort to know that he was on guard, small but if necessary very noisy, through the dark night. She summed up her feelings for her dog in a simple sentence. 'He's a good friend to me.'

The Lord God said 'It is not good that man should be alone; I will make him a helper fit for him'. So the Lord God formed every beast of the field and every bird of the air, and brought them to the man.

Genesis 2:18-19

. . . whilst this appealing King Charles Cavalier pup looks ready for another nap

Strong Love

He was a dear old man, always smiling and welcoming. Visiting him was a treat because he made you feel special, an honoured guest. If you had good news his face would light up with delight. He listened lovingly to your troubles and gave wise advice if you asked for it. He enjoyed a good laugh more than anything. Serene and peaceful, you would think his life had been a bed of roses. Not a bit of it. His childhood had been desolate, his marriage very difficult, his health was poor. But somehow all the hard experiences, which would have made some people bitter, had strengthened his loving nature. His was a strong love because it had been tempered in the fire.

Love is patient and kind; love is not jealous or boastful; it is not arrogant or rude. Love does not insist on its own way; it is not irritable or resentful; it does not rejoice at wrong, but rejoices in the right. Love bears all things, believes all things, hopes all things, endures all things.

1. Corinthians 13:4-7

Window shopping at Chislehurst, London

Fishing is still a way of life at Looe in Cornwall

Live Peaceably

'Remember to say 'please' and 'thank you' and 'thank you for having me' when you go home'. We try to teach children manners – how to behave politely. How often do we adults remember to be polite? It is easy to be courteous to our friends, the people we like. But what about people we don't like? What about people who are rude to us? There is a story about a great man who had an encounter with someone who was very offensive to him. To the surprise of those watching he replied politely to his insulter.

'How could you lower yourself by answering that wretch so gently?' one asked.

'Am I to let him teach me how to behave?' was the reply.

Repay no one evil for evil, but take thought for what is noble in the sight of all. If possible, so far as it depends upon you, live peaceably with all.

Romans 12:16,17

Looking down on Bedruthan Steps in North Cornwall

Friends

What gives you the greatest happiness? Most people would probably answer 'I am happiest when I am with people I love, people I know love me. I feel secure then, most myself. I know I can depend on loving members of my family and old friends who know me and understand my ways.'

When love is missing, when friends are far away, loneliness can bring unhappiness. How can we cope then? Who are we to turn to? One way is to look for other lonely people. Sadly, they are not hard to find. A knock on a door, a birthday card, just a smile in a shop can be the beginning of friendship. And in the loneliest times it's good to remember that there is one friend who never lets us down, who is always near, always loving.

If God is for us, who is against us? He who did not spare his own Son but gave him up for us all, will he not also give us all things with him?

Romans 8:31-32

Glorious Autumn colours – at Hartsop Beck in Cumbria . . .

. . . and Clapham in North Yorkshire

Harter Fell casts morning reflections on Hawes Water, Cumbria

Surprises

The coach journey had become rather boring, the scenery uninteresting and the sky overcast. Suddenly, round a bend in the road, the whole prospect changed. The view opened up into a spectacular scene. The sun came out, brightening every colour. Everyone cheered up and looked around with delight and thankfulness.

When pleasant surprises come on the journey through life we can be encouraged by them. They can be reminders that we are surrounded by God's love. His love is not fitful, like the sun, but constant, from moment to moment, even through the dullest of days.

I have loved you with an everlasting love;
therefore I have continued my faithfulness to you.

Jeremiah 31:3

Stunning sunset at Ullapool, Highland

Listening

There comes a time in life when the pace has to slow down. We just cannot rush around as we once did. Now we need longer spaces to rest and recover our energy. Maybe we are more or less immobile. There is a terrible temptation to believe we are no longer any use to anyone because we can't get around easily. But whoever said that people are only valued for their physical activity? One of the things most needed in these days is people with time to listen. Listen to the joys and fears and hopes of the young. Listen to the sad yearnings of the bereaved. Listen to the lonely. Earn a reputation as a good listener, and the world will beat a path to your door.

Welcome one another, therefore, as Christ has welcomed you, for the glory of God.

Romans 15:7

Colourful displays in Bank Street, Galashiels, Borders

ISBN 0-7117-0417-1 © Jarrold Publishing 1989. Reprinted 1993. Designed and produced by Parke Sutton Limited for Jarrold Publishing, Norwich. Printed in Portugal. 2/93